The U.S.

MW00974335

DISCARDED

The U.S. Armed Forces
The U.S. Navy SEALs

by Angie Peterson Kaelberer

Consultant:
Barbara J. Fox
Reading Specialist
North Carolina State University

Capstone press

Mankato, Minnesota

Blazers is published by Capstone Press,
151 Good Counsel Drive, P.O. Box 669, Mankato, Minnesota 56002.
www.capstonepress.com

Library of Congress Cataloging-in-Publication Data
Kaelberer, Angie Peterson.
   The U.S. Navy SEALs / by Angie Peterson Kaelberer.
      p. cm.—(Blazers. The U.S. Armed Forces)
   Includes bibliographical references and index.
   ISBN 0-7368-3794-9 (hardcover)
   1. United States. Navy. SEALs—Juvenile literature. I. Title. II. Series.
VG87.K34 2005
359.9'84—dc22   2004016186

Summary: Describes the missions, weapons, and equipment of the
U.S. Navy SEALs.

Credits

Juliette Peters, set designer; Enoch Peterson and Steve Christensen,
   book designers; Jo Miller, photo researcher; Scott Thoms, photo editor

Photo Credits

Corbis/Jim Sugar, cover (background); Leif Skoogfors, 20
Corel, cover (foreground)
DVIC/CW02 Charles Grow, USMC, 15; PH2 Shane McCoy, USN, 28–29;
   TSGT Brian Snyder, USAF, 5, 6–7, 9
Navy Photo by PH1 Andy McKaskle, 11; PH1 Arlo K. Abrahamson, 21, 23
   (bottom); PH1 Tim Turner, 13; PH2 Eric S. Logsdon, 16–17, 23 (top);
   PH2 Michael J. Pusnik, Jr., 19; PH3 John DeCoursey, 22, 25
Photo by U.S. Air Force/Staff Sgt. Aaron D. Allmon II, 26; Tech Sgt.
   Scott Reed, 12

**Capstone Press thanks Mark Wertheimer of the Naval Historical Center in
Washington, D.C., for his assistance with this book.**

1 2 3 4 5 6 10 09 08 07 06 05

Table of Contents

★★★★★★★★★★★★★

U.S. Navy SEALs in Action

United States Navy SEALs huddle in a boat in an enemy country. The boat moves toward the shore.

The SEALs dive into the cold water. They quickly swim toward the shore. Other Navy members watch for enemies.

The SEALs move toward the beach. They are ready to check for explosive weapons called land mines.

BLAZER FACT

Only men can be SEALs. Congress doesn't allow women to serve as SEALs.

Weapons and Equipment

Many SEAL missions involve water. SEALs are skilled divers. They use scuba gear to breathe underwater.

Scuba gear

M-4 rifle

M-4 rifle

SEALs carry weapons during
missions. They often use lightweight
M-4 rifles. The rifles can hit targets as far
away as 2,000 feet (610 meters).

SEALs use electronic equipment to communicate. They send information to SEAL teams around the world.

BLAZER FACT

In their fourth week of training, SEAL trainees sleep only four hours during a five-day period.

Special Operations Craft Riverine

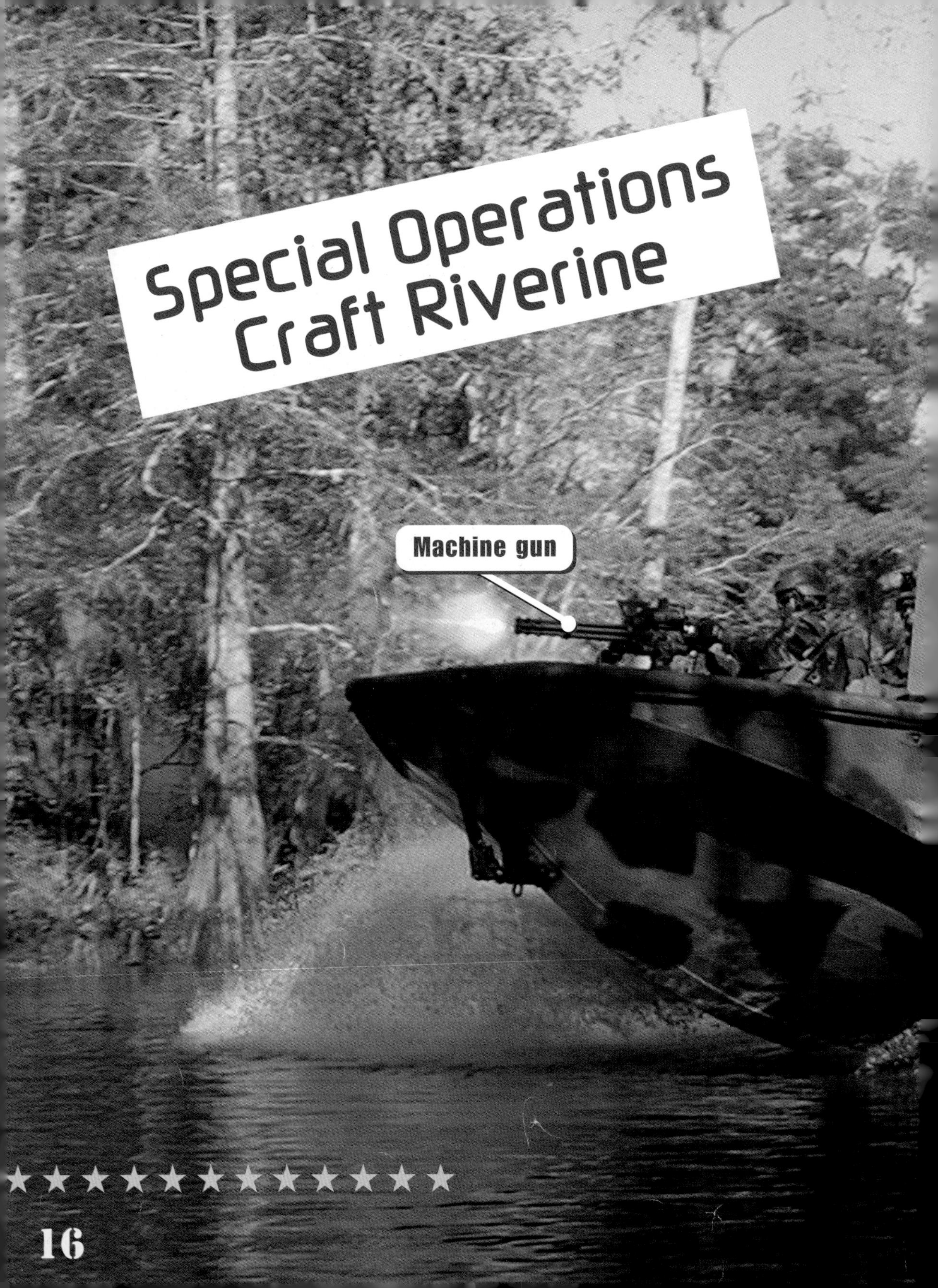

Radar

Armored hull

Vehicles

SEALs need to quickly reach mission sites. They sometimes drop by rope from Seahawk helicopters.

Desert Patrol Vehicles (DPVs) help SEALs get around on land. The small dune buggies roll easily over sand.

Desert Patrol Vehicle

Machine gun

Grenade launcher

BLAZER FACT

Rudy Boesch from *Survivor* and former Minnesota Governor Jesse Ventura both served as SEALs.

Rigid Hull Inflatable Boats carry SEALs to mission sites. The Special Operations Craft Riverine travels quickly on rivers. SEALs use the MARK V Special Operations Craft near ocean shores.

Special Operations Craft Riverine

MARK V Special Operations Craft

SEAL Missions

A SEAL team has six platoons. Two officers and 14 enlisted members are in a platoon. Officers lead enlisted members.

★ ★ ★ ★ ★ ★ ★ ★ ★

SEALs rescue missing or hurt soldiers. They gather information about enemy forces. SEALs help make the world a safer place.

NAVY RANKS

★ ★ ★ ★ ★ ★ ★ ★ ★ ★ ★ ★ ★ ★ ★ ★

ENLISTED	OFFICERS
Seaman	Ensign
Petty Officer	Lieutenant
	Commander
	Captain
	Admiral

SEALs defend an aircraft carrier

Glossary

enlisted member (en-LISS-tuhd MEM-bur)—a member of the military who is not an officer

land mine (LAND MINE)—a bomb buried underground

mission (MISH-uhn)—a military task

officer (OF-uh-sur)—a military member who directs enlisted members in their duties

platoon (pluh-TOON)—a small group of soldiers who work together

scuba (SKOO-buh)—self-contained underwater breathing apparatus

weapon (WEP-un)—anything used when fighting; guns, tanks, and bombs are weapons.

Read More

Donovan, Sandy. *U.S. Naval Special Warfare Forces.* U.S. Armed Forces. Minneapolis: Lerner, 2005.

Green, Michael, and Gladys Green. *The U.S. Navy SEALs at War.* On the Front Lines. Mankato, Minn.: Capstone Press, 2004.

Kennedy, Robert C. *Life with the Navy SEALs.* On Duty. New York: Children's Press, 2000.

Internet Sites

FactHound offers a safe, fun way to find Internet sites related to this book. All of the sites on FactHound have been researched by our staff.

Here's how:

1. Visit *www.facthound.com*
2. Type in this special code **0736837949** for age-appropriate sites. Or enter a search word related to this book for a more general search.
3. Click on the **Fetch It** button.

FactHound will fetch the best sites for you!

Index